Talents

Chelsea Kong

© 2021 CHELSEA KONG

ALL RIGHTS RESERVED. ALL IMAGES USED IN THIS BOOK ARE LICENSED COPIES FROM THEIR RESPECTFUL OWNERS INCLUDING FREEPIK. THIS BOOK OR ANY PORTION THEREOF MAY NOT BE REPRODUCED OR USED IN ANY MANNER WHATSOEVER WITHOUT THE EXPRESS WRITTEN PERMISSION OF THE PUBLISHER EXCEPT FOR THE USE OF BRIEF QUOTATIONS IN A BOOK REVIEW.

PRINTED IN 2021, MADE IN TORONTO, CANADA
ISBN: 978-1-9903996-4-0
LIBRARY AND ARCHIVES CANADA

YOU ARE SPECIAL!

GOD GIVES EACH OF US SPECIAL GIFTS.
WE ARE MADE DIFFERENT FOR HIS GLORY.
WE NEED TO ACCEPT THE GIFTS.

TALENTS

A SPECIAL GIFT THAT GOD GIVES US.
EACH PERSON HAS ONE OR MORE GIFTS.
USE THESE TO SHOW PEOPLE THAT GOD IS REAL.

TALENTS IN THE BIBLE

"ALL WHO ARE SKILLED AMONG YOU ARE TO COME AND MAKE EVERYTHING THE LORD HAS COMMANDED: (EXODUS 35:10)

FOR WE ARE GOD'S HANDIWORK, CREATED IN CHRIST JESUS TO DO GOOD WORKS, WHICH GOD PREPARED IN ADVANCE FOR US TO DO (EPHESIANS 2:10).

GOD WILL DO IT!

"ALL WHO ARE SKILLED AMONG YOU ARE TO COME AND MAKE EVERYTHING THE LORD HAS COMMANDED:
(EXODUS 35:10)

HE WILL BRING US BEFORE THE MIGHTY.
HE WILL GIVE US THE POWER, WISDOM,
AND SPIRIT TO MAKE ANYTHING HE WANTS.

THE OLD TESTAMENT

JOSEPH IS GOOD AT EVERYTHING HE DID AND HE BECAME THE PRIME MINISTER OF EGYPT.

BEZALEL AND OHOLIAB HAVE GIFTS IN MAKING ALL THINGS FOR THE TABERNACLE.

DAVID PLAYED THE LYRE BEFORE KING SAUL AND WAS A SHEPHERD. LATER DAVID BECAME KING OF ISRAEL.

KING SOLOMON HAS WISDOM TO BUILD THE TEMPLE, WRITE SONGS, POEMS, AND JUDGE ISRAEL.
DANIEL AND HIS FRIENDS WERE GIVEN WITH THE WISE MEN.
PROVERBS 31 WOMAN HAS MANY TALENTS.

THE NEW TESTAMENT

THE APOSTLES ARE FISHERMEN.
DORCAS MADE ROBES, CLOTHING, AND MORE.
PAUL MADE TENTS AND IS AN APOSTLE.

KNOW YOUR TALENTS

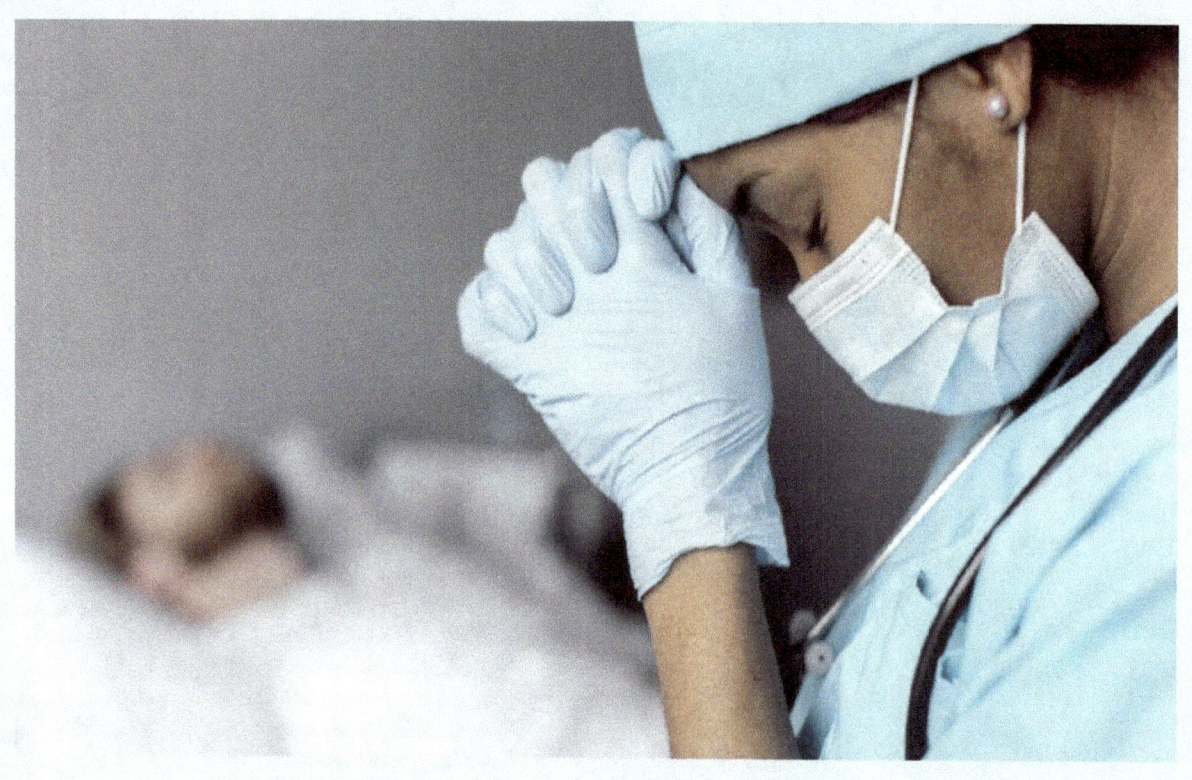

FIND OUT WHAT YOU ARE GOOD AT DOING.
TAKE TIME TO USE YOUR GIFTS EVERY DAY.
ONE DAY YOU WILL MEET PEOPLE, MIGHTY PEOPLE.

SEEK GOD

WORSHIP, PRAISE, AND THANK HIM.
DANCE WITH JOY.
PRAY EVERY DAY.
LISTEN, DO, AND GO
WHERE HE TELLS YOU.

PRAY

ASK GOD WHAT HE WANTS YOU TO DO.
HE WILL SHOW YOU WHO, WHERE, AND HOW TO USE YOUR GIFTS.
HOLY SPIRIT CAN HELP YOU GROW YOUR GIFTS.
GOD CAN GIVE YOU IDEAS AND FIND OUT WHAT HE WANTS YOU TO DO.

OTHER TALENTS

THE GIFT IS PROPHESYING, FAITH, SERVING, TEACHING, ENCOURAGING, GIVING A LOT, LEADING RIGHTLY, AND SHOWING MERCY BEING HAPPY (ROMANS 12:6-8).
SUPPLY NEEDS AND GIVES THANKS (2 CORINTHIANS 9:12).

FAMILY

Honor your father and your mother, so you can live long (Exodus 20:12).

Children are a heritage from the Lord, offspring a reward from him (Psalm 127:3).

Families should have one heart and mind in God to work together every day.

EDUCATION

Train the child to walk with God and teach a man (Proverbs 22:6, 9:9).
God gives teachers the wisdom to teach.
The teacher must know how to teach and correct mistakes.
God's word should be taught (2 Timothy 3:16).

GOVERNMENT

DANIEL AND JOSEPH WERE PRIME MINISTERS. THERE ARE ALSO PRESIDENTS, PREMIER, MAYOR, MPS, MPPS, COUNCILORS, AND TREASURERS.

GOVERNMENT OFFICE

GOD CHOSE THE LEADERS AND THOSE WHO RULE OVER US, SO WE MUST HONOUR THEM AND PRAY FOR THEM (ROMANS 13:1, 1 TIMOTHY 2:1-3).

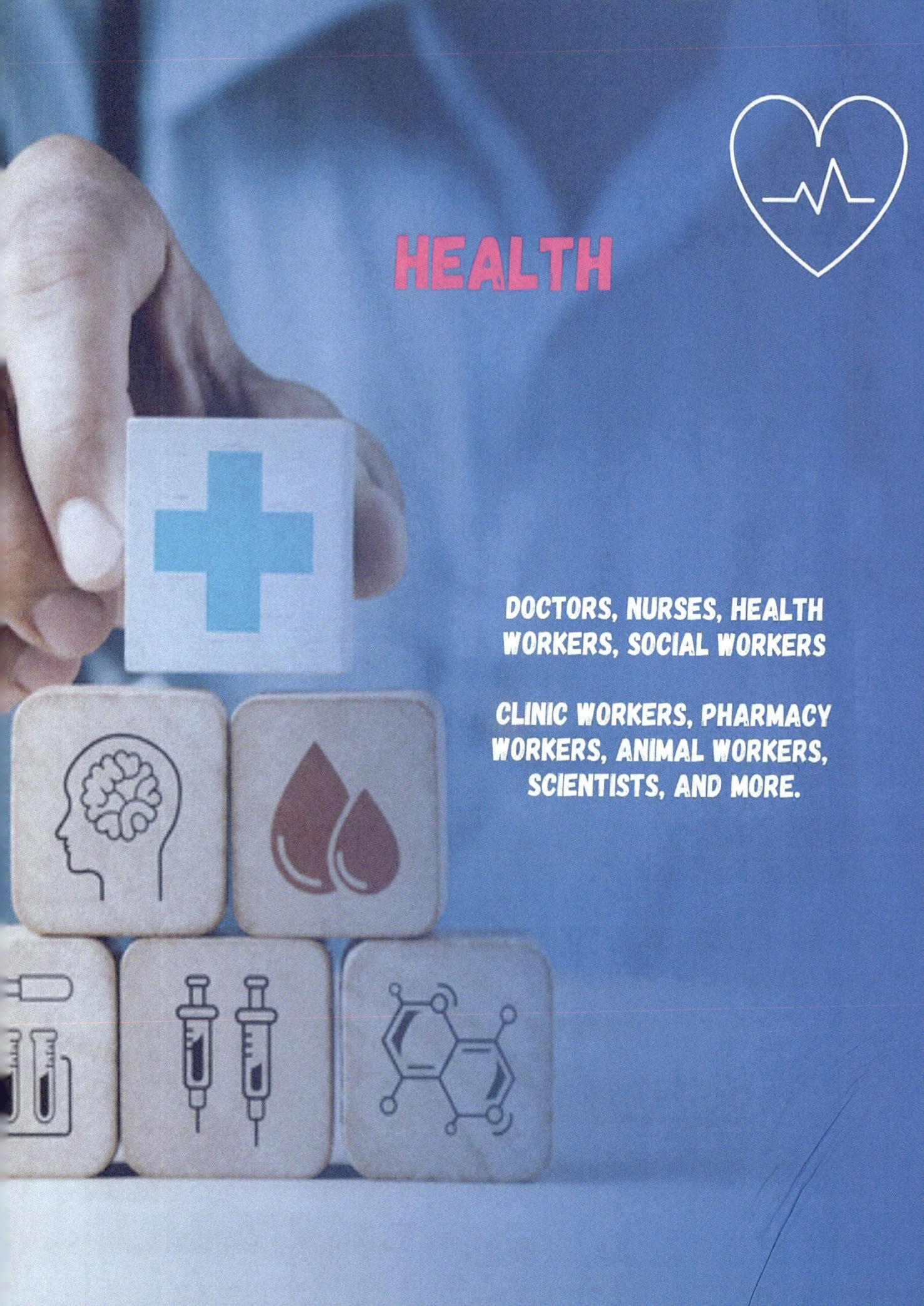

THIS IS PART OF THE GOVERNMENT.
THEY ALSO NEED GOD'S WISDOM AND POWER TO HELP SAVE PEOPLE THAT ARE SICK OR WANT TO STAY HEALTHY.

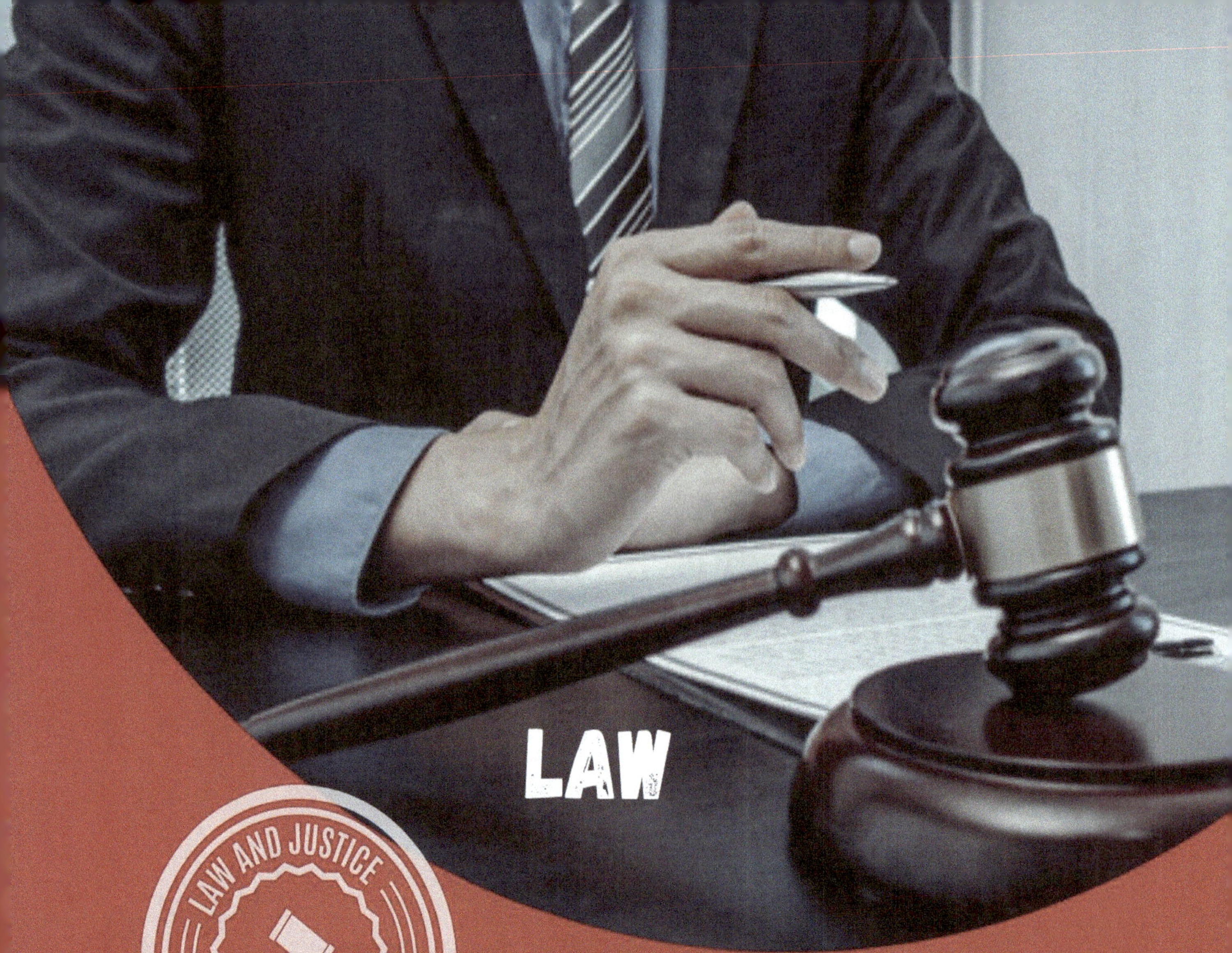

LAW

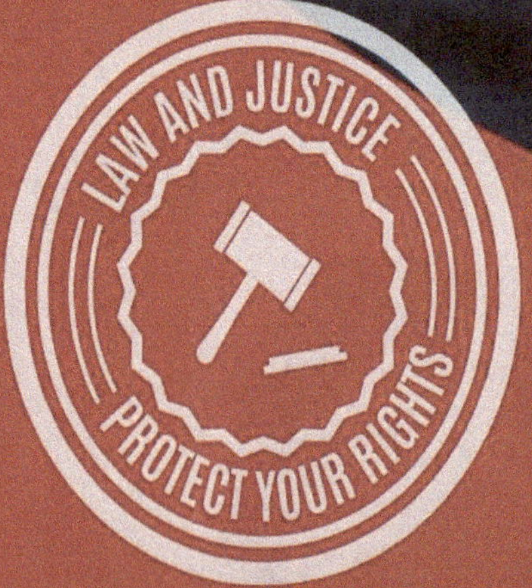
LAW AND JUSTICE
PROTECT YOUR RIGHTS

JUDGES, LAWYERS, LAW CLERKS, POLICE, OFFICERS, FIREMEN, PARKING, SECURITY, CONSULTANT, AND MORE.

LAW

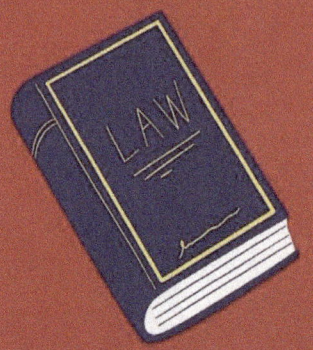

GOD HAS SET THE LAW IN OUR COUNTRY, PROVINCE, AND CITY.
WE NEED TO LEARN TO FOLLOW THE LAWS THAT GOD SET FOR US.
WE ALSO HAVE TO LIVE WITH THE RULES WHERE WE LIVE.

MEDIA

THIS IS NEWS, TECHNOLOGY, PHOTOGRAPHY, DIGITAL MEDIA, BROADCASTING (RADIO AND TELEVISION), AND ADVERTISING. WE MUST GIVE THE TRUTH TO PEOPLE.

ARTS

DESIGNERS, CARPENTERS, BUILDERS, AND MORE.
IT GIVES US PEACE IN OUR MINDS AND HEART.
WE CAN MAKE OUR CLOTHES AND THINGS.

BUSINESS

YOU CAN HAVE A BUSINESS THAT YOU WANT AND LIKE.
LEARN FROM PEOPLE WHO OWN THEIR BUSINESS.

YOU NEED TO KNOW HOW TO USE MONEY.
GOD'S WORD HAS THE KEYS TO DO BUSINESS WELL.

OTHER

THERE ARE DRIVERS TO GIVE PEOPLE RIDES TO GO PLACES.
REMEMBER THE FARMERS AND THOSE WHO CLEAN.

HONOUR GOD

WE MUST HONOUR GOD ALL THE TIME (PHILIPPIANS 4:8). HONOR THE LORD WITH YOUR WEALTH, WITH THE FIRSTFRUITS OF ALL YOUR CROPS; (PROVERBS 3:9).

WORK HARD IN ALL YOU DO IN WHAT GOD GIVES YOU AND YOU WILL GET THE REWARD (2 CHRONICLES 31:21).

SALVATION PRAYER

God, I know I sinned against you. Forgive me for the wrong that I have done. I believe that Jesus Christ died on the cross for me. That He rose from the grave so that after three days. I can have His long-lasting life. Come into my heart to be my Lord and Savior. I choose to turn away from my sins and I choose to follow you. Lead me to walk with you. Keep me safe and teach me your ways. Stop every bad thing in my life that has an open door to hurt me. Close those doors. Holy Spirit fill me now in Jesus' name. Amen.

BAPTISM IN THE HOLY SPIRIT

Jesus, you are the one that fills me with Your Spirit. Come Holy Spirit and come into my life and fill me to overflow with Your presence. Come with your fire too. Thank you for the gift of tongues in Jesus' name. Amen.

Open your mouth and let the words come out that God gives you. It will be words that you don't know what they mean. You can ask God what it means. You need to let Him talk through you every day to grow this gift.

He will bring you closer to God and you will know Jesus more. You will have power from God to do great things and know things.

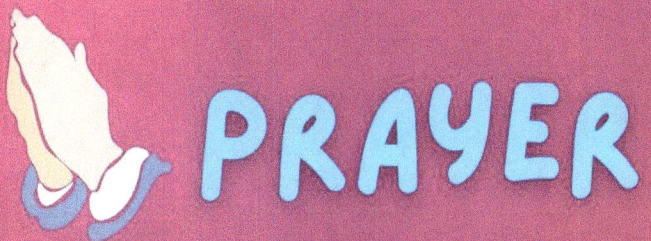 # PRAYER

Father, teach me what my talents are and how to use them for you. Bring me to the people and places you want me to go. Give me ideas and wisdom to use them. I want to give you glory in all that I do in Jesus' name. Amen.

Message from the Author

Our talents are God's gifts to us to show His power in our life. God wants us to be close to Him when we use them. It will help us to tell others about Jesus Christ. We need to remember it is God that gives us the gifts. We are to take care of them and use them. Everyone has different talents, so we can bless each other. We must accept what God gives to us is the best.

OTHER PRODUCTS

Knowing God
How to Hear God's Voice
New Life in Jesus
Loving Israel
God's Gifts/Spiritual Talents
Meeting God
Word Power
Fruit of the Spirit
The Tabernacle
Bride for Jesus
A Life of Prayer
Live Free
Who am I in Jesus
Walk in Love
God's Favor
Man of God
Woman of God
How to Use Money
God's Wisdom
Fasting
See Jerusalem and Bethany
First Fruit Offering

Feast of Trumpets
Day of Atonement
Feast of Tabernacles
Counting the Omer
Festival of Lights
Glory, Presence, and Holy Spirit
Live in God's Presence
Pentecost
See Galilee, Nazareth, and Tiberias
Hear God Speak
Knowing Jesus
Knowing Holy Spirit
A Healthy Life and Healthy Life Work Book

OTHER PRODUCTS

Devotionals
31 Day Devotional

Puzzle Books
Biblical Puzzle Book Vol 1-5

Bible Puzzles for Young Children Book 1-3

Biblical Puzzle for Children Books 1-5

Teaching Series
How to Hear God's Voice Teaching Guide & Audio Book

Relationship with God, Jesus, Holy Spirit Guide

Knowing God, Jesus, Holy Spirit Guide & Audio Book

Flowing in the Prophetic

Teaching (Non-Sale on my website)

Purim

Passover

Resurrection

More books to come!

BOOK REVIEWS

More books on Amazon, Kobo, and Barnes and Noble.
https://chelseak532002550.wordpress.com/

> More books on Amazon, Kobo, and Barnes and Noble, Smashwords, and IngramSpark.
> https://www.amazon.com/author/chelseakong
>
> Please leave a review and share with friends to help the author continue to write more books to reach more readers. Thank you so much for your support.

Review!

About
CHELSEA KONG

She is a writer, creative arts and digital media artist, skilled administration and payroll professional, and podcaster. Chelsea also served in a variety of roles, from audiovisual, photography, to assisting on the worship team, and ministry team. She also has a passion for families being united.

Chelsea graduated from Hotel and Restaurant Management, Digital Media Arts, Office Administration, Payroll Professional, and experience working with children. Chelsea lives in Toronto, Canada. She mainly writes children's books, stories, bridal writing, poems, lyrics for songs, words of encouragement, blessings, prayers, and jokes. The author of How to Hear the Voice of God, the Bridal Collection, Knowing God, etc. She also has her own Bible Puzzle books and other inspired products. Her podcast channel is called Chelsea K on Anchor, Spotify, and iTunes.

Please check my website to find out more:
https://chelseak532002550.wordpress.com/

THANK YOU FOR PURCHASING THIS BOOK,
JUST TO SHOW MY APPRECIATION:
HTTPS://CHELSEAK532002550.WORDPRESS.COM/BOOKS-FOR-SHARING/